@RosenTeenTalk

BULLYING

Jodyanne Benson

ROSEN
PUBLISHING

NEW YORK

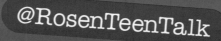
@RosenTeenTalk

BULLYING

Jodyanne Benson

ROSEN
PUBLISHING

NEW YORK

Published in 2021 by The Rosen Publishing Group, Inc.
29 East 21st Street, New York, NY 10010

Editor: Elizabeth Krajnik
Designer: Michael Flynn
Interior Layout: Rachel Rising

Photo Credits: Cover, pp. 1, 3, 45 GagliardiPhotography/Shutterstock.com; Cover, p. 41 Cosmic_Design/Shutterstock.com; Cover, pp. 1, 6, 8, 10, 14, 16, 18, 22, 24, 26, 32, 34, 36, 38, 42 Vitya_M/Shutterstock.com; pp. 3, 5 fizkes/Shutterstock.com; pp. 3, 13 PhotoAlto/Dinoco Greco/Getty Images; pp. 3, 21 Syda Productions/Shutterstock.com; pp. 3, 31 LightField Studios/Shutterstock.com; pp. 3, 40, 43 Rawpixel.com/Shutterstock.com; p. 6 Brycia James/E+/Getty Images; p. 8 Africa Studio/Shutterstock.com; p. 10 Constantinis/E+/Getty Images; p. 11 Khosro/Shutterstock.com; p. 14 Andreas Stamm/Getty Images; p. 15 Stockbyte/Getty Images; p. 17 fstop123/E+/Getty Images; p. 19 Rayman/Photodisc/Getty Images; p. 22 Daisy Daisy/Shutterstock.com; p. 23 bearsky23/Shutterstock.com; p. 25 Olimpik/Shutterstock.com; p. 26 Maskot/Getty Images; p. 26, 28 SpeedKingz/Shutterstock.com; p. 29 leungchopan/Shutterstock.com; p. 32 Lurin/Shutterstock.com; p. 34 Halfdark/Getty Images; p. 35 monticello/Shuttterstock.com; p. 36 Thinkstock/Stockbyte/Getty Images; p. 37 George Rudy/Shutterstock.com; p. 38 New Africa/Shutterstock.com; p. 39 Antonio Guillem/Shutterstock.com; p. 40, 43 Rawpixel.com/Shutterstock.com; p. 41 SMAK_Photo/Shutterstock.com; p. 43 scoutori/Shutterstock.com.

Some of the images in this book illustrate individuals who are models. The depictions do not imply actual situations or events.

Cataloging-in-Publication Data

Names: Benson, Jodyanne.
Title: Bullying / Jodyanne Benson.
Description: New York : Rosen Publishing, 2021. | Series: @RosenTeenTalk | Includes glossary and index.
Identifiers: ISBN 9781499468007 (pbk.) | ISBN 9781499468014 (library bound)
Subjects: LCSH: Bullying--Juvenile literature. | Cyberbullying--Juvenile literature. | Bullying--Prevention--Juvenile literature.
Classification: LCC BF637.B85 B48 2021 | DDC 302.34'3--dc23

Manufactured in the United States of America

CPSIA Compliance Information: Batch #BSR20. For further information contact Rosen Publishing, New York, New York at 1-800-237-9932.

Find us on

CONTENTS

Finding a Place

When I was 13 years old, I went to a new scho[ol] [o]f kids there had the newest clothes and cell pho[nes] [I] didn't have any of those things. I think that's w[hat] [mad]e it hard for me to find friends.

The popular girls in my class were very good at [sport]s. But I've always liked music and acting more. [It se]emed like no one at my new school shared [my i]nterests.

Soon after I started at my new school, the pop[ular girls] began talking about me behind my back and ca[lled me] [w]eird. They made fun of me. They wouldn't invi[te me] [t]o sit with them during lunch or study hall. I'd n[ever] [bee]n alone before. Why me?

Mia's a great person. But she feels sad and lonely when she's bullied.

Chapter 2

WHAT IS BULLYING?

Bullying is when someone scares, hurts, or **threatens** a smaller or weaker person. Bullies use their power and popularity to make people feel small.

Bullying often happens at school and on the bus. It also happens on the internet. However, bullying can happen anywhere and at any time.

One person alone or a group of people can bully someone.

Fact!

Verbal and social bullying are the most common types of bullying.

There are three types of bullying. Verbal bullying is saying or writing mean things about someone. Social bullying is hurting the way other people think about someone. Physical bullying is hurting someone's body or belongings.

EXAMPLES OF BULLYING

Verbal Bullying

- Teasing
- Taunting
- Inappropriate sexual comments
- Name-calling
- Threatening

Social Bullying

- Leaving someone out on purpose
- Telling others not to be friends with someone
- Spreading rumors about someone
- Embarrassing someone in front of others

Physical Bullying

- Hitting, kicking, or punching
- Tripping or pushing
- Taking or breaking someone's belongings
- Spitting
- Making mean gestures

WHO IS PART OF BULLYING?

People get involved in bullying for different reasons and in different ways. Sometimes people who were bullied previously begin bullying others.

Sometimes people help the person who bullies. They do this by **reinforcing** the bullying behavior. They might laugh or support the person who bullies in different ways.

About 29 percent of middle school students experience bullying in school hallways or near lockers.

Witnesses are people who see bullying happening. Outsiders are people who see bullying happening but don't get involved in the situation. People who defend get involved in bullying situations.

Facts and Figures

About 30 percent of young people say they've bullied others.

About 70 percent of young people say they've seen bullying in their schools.

WAYS TO AVOID LABELING

Labeling someone a "bully" or a "victim" can be hurtful too. Instead of labeling the person, label the person's behavior:

- Instead of "bully," try calling them "the person who bullied."
- Instead of "victim," try calling them "the person who was bullied."

WHO GETS BULLIED?

People bully others for many reasons. They may have problems at home. Bullying others is how they deal with **stressful** and **traumatic** things. They may bully someone just for being different.

Boys are more likely to bully others than girls. This is because boys are often raised not to talk about their feelings and to be tough.

Some groups of people are more likely to be bullied than others. People with disabilities, people who aren't very social, and people in the **LGBTQ** community are often bullied. To someone who bullies, these people may seem weak. They often can't stick up for themselves.

WHO BECOMES A BULLY?

Children who bully may be popular and like to be in control. Other children who bully may not have many friends and may have low self-esteem. Children who show these signs are more likely to bully others:

- **Aggressive** behavior
- Issues at home
- Think other people are often bad
- Have a hard time following rules
- Think violence is OK
- Have friends who bully others
- Have been bullied in the past

Chapter 3

From a Bully to a Friend

I've bullied others for as long as I can remember. I didn't know why I bullied others and I never thought it would be possible to stop.

In ninth grade, I started bullying an **exchange** student. He seemed so different from my friends and me. It made me uncomfortable. Instead of getting to know him, I called him names, pushed him into the lockers, and stole his backpack.

One day, the school **counselor** called me to her office. She explained that the reason I bully others might be because I'm trying to control situations that make me scared or uncomfortable. She helped me find ways to control my anger and deal with stress. I'm working to become friends with the exchange student.

Even if someone dresses, acts, or talks differently from you, they don't deserve to be bullied. They deserve kindness and respect.

WARNING SIGNS

Children who are bullied often show warning signs. They may have a hard time sleeping or have nightmares. They may also have injuries they can't explain. Their belongings may be damaged or even lost.

Children who bully also show warning signs. They often blame others for their problems. They may also worry about their **reputation**.

Fact!

Data from 2011 shows that only about 20 to 30 percent of children who were bullied told an adult.

Children who are bullied may start getting bad grades. They may try to avoid going to school. It's also common for children who are bullied to feel sick or helpless. In the worst cases, children who are bullied may hurt themselves or run away.

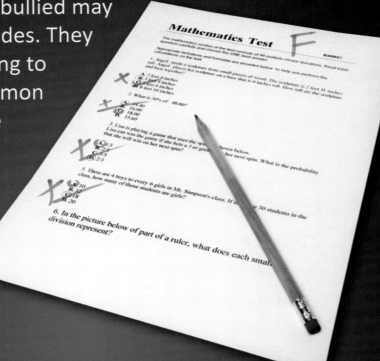

SCARED TO ASK FOR HELP

Children who are bullied are often too scared to tell a trusted adult or ask for help for a number of reasons:

- They feel helpless or want to handle it alone.
- They don't want to be a tattletale.
- They're afraid the bully will find out.
- They're embarrassed.
- They feel like no one understands.

FEAR OF DIFFERENCES

Children who bully often target people because they're different. They may have a different skin color. They may be from a different country. They may speak a different language. Often times, children who bully don't understand these differences and are afraid of them.

Children often bully others with different religious beliefs because they are misinformed about that religion. Children may bully Muslim students because they think all Muslims are **terrorists**.

Fact!

Bullying isn't illegal. Each state government handles bullying differently. The **federal** government doesn't have an antibullying law.

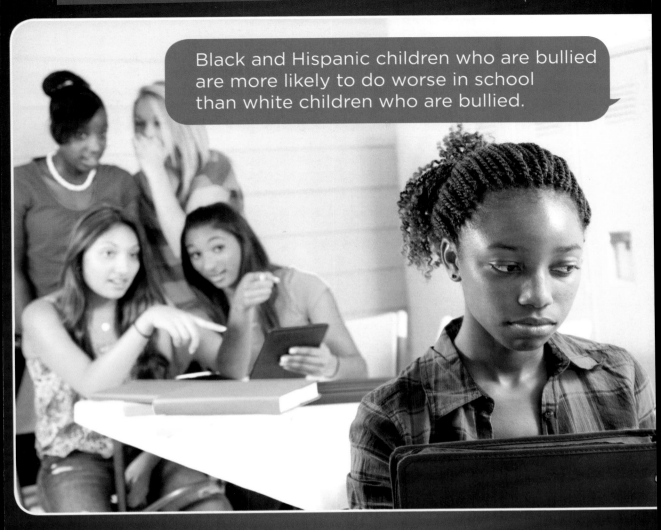

Black and Hispanic children who are bullied are more likely to do worse in school than white children who are bullied.

GETTING THE LAW INVOLVED

Harassment is when bullying happens often and is serious. The federal government has laws that protect people from harassment. Getting the law involved is important. This helps make sure people are being treated fairly.

DISABILITIES AND SPECIAL NEEDS

Children with disabilities are more likely to be bullied. They may not be able to stick up for themselves. They may also not have friends to stick up for them. It's often harder for these children to find their place.

Children who bully may also target children who have special health needs, such as diabetes or a food allergy. The child who bullies may make fun of them. They may even try to make the other person sick on purpose. This can be very dangerous.

Holding a sports night for children with physical disabilities can help school staff and students understand their needs. This may keep them from becoming the target of bullying.

Chapter 4

Challenges at School

I have a learning disability called dyslexia. I've always had a hard time in school. I struggle the most with reading and spelling. I get very anxious when I'm asked to read out loud in class. I often mix words up or say them incorrectly.

Kids in my English class would make fun of me. They'd mimic me and call me stupid. I never wanted to go to school. I would pretend to be sick so I wouldn't have to go. I started getting bad grades.

One day, I talked to my friends about being bullied. I explained to them what it's like to have a learning disability. They started sticking up for me. Soon after, the bullies left me alone.

Telling people you trust about being bullied can make you feel less frustrated and alone.

WHAT IS CYBERBULLYING?

Cyberbullying is bullying that uses devices, such as a cellphone or computer. It can take place on social media sites and apps, such as Facebook, Instagram, Snapchat, and Twitter. Examples of cyberbullying include sending hurtful text messages or posting a mean picture of someone online.

Cyberbullying can cause the person who's being bullied to live in a constant state of fear.

If someone posts a hurtful video of someone and refuses to delete it, this is also cyberbullying. Sometimes, cyberbullies get in trouble with the law.

STEPS TO TAKE

If you're being cyberbullied, following these steps might help you get the bullying behavior to stop:

- Tell a trusted adult about the cyberbullying. In some cases, you may need to tell the police.

- Don't respond to or forward messages from cyberbullies.

- Keep **evidence** of the bullying.

- Report cyberbullying to the social media site it took place on or your phone service or email provider.

- Block the cyberbully.

- Change all your passwords to keep yourself safe.

HATERS GONNA HATE

A "hater" is someone who says hurtful things about people to make them look or feel bad. Being a hater is another kind of bullying. Haters may target people in person or online. A hater may be someone you don't know.

Haters also often target people who are different from them. To deal with a hater, you can follow the same steps as dealing with a cyberbully. Haters gonna hate. This means you should ignore the haters. Just keep being yourself!

> Even if you have a hater, you should still be nice to them. Haters don't actually hate you. Their behavior may mean they're upset with things in their own life.

LET'S STOP BULLYING

As long as someone knows what bullying is, they can spot it and stop it. They may even be able to keep it from happening in the future. If you or someone you know is being bullied, it's important to talk to a trusted adult. They'll be able to help you.

Your parents are more likely to be able to help you if you keep them updated on your life. Tell them about how your day was and if anything bad happened.

You can stand up for someone who's being bullied. Tell the person who's bullying to stop. If the person who's bullying them doesn't listen, you can help the person being bullied walk away.

Important Questions

Do you know what bullying is and isn't?

Why do you think people bully?

Whom would you tell about bullying?

Have you ever felt scared at school because of bullying?

Do you see bullying taking place? What do you do?

What do you think parents and teachers can do to help stop bullying?

DID YOU KNOW?

If you see bullying taking place at your school, you can start an antibullying club. Ask your classmates—even those who bully—to join. Find a teacher to help you run it.

BEING A BYSTANDER

A bystander is someone who sees bullying taking place. Bystanders exist in person and online. Anyone can be a bystander—friends, parents, teachers, and strangers.

You can be an upstander online. If you see someone being bullied, step in and try to stop the bullying behavior. You can report the behavior to keep it from happening again.

Being a bystander means the person doesn't act on the bullying behavior. They don't take the side of the person who bullies. However, they don't stick up for the person being bullied either. They might be afraid of becoming a target. However, doing nothing might tell the person who bullies that their behavior is OK.

DID YOU KNOW?

When bystanders step in, bullying stops within 10 seconds 57 percent of the time.

BECOME AN UPSTANDER

An upstander is someone who tries to stop bullying. Here are things upstanders might do in a bullying situation:

- Change the subject.
- Use humor.
- Include others.
- Question the bullying behavior.
- Report bullying behavior.
- Protect people who are bullied.
- Talk about your differences and highlight how differences are good.

Chapter 5

From Bystander to Upstander

I believe everyone deserves to be included and treated with kindness. However, my actions didn't always **reflect** my beliefs. Many of my friends were popular. They bullied kids for just about any reason. Even though I didn't bully people, I watched my friends bully others.

One day, my friends stole someone's notebook. They wrote mean and hurtful things inside. I had had enough. I took the notebook away from them. I crossed out everything they wrote and put my own note inside. It said, "Want to sit with me at lunch?"

After that, I decided to find better friends. I realized good friends don't bully people. I started standing up for people who are being bullied. I'm happy I chose to be an upstander.

Choosing to become an upstander shows other bystanders that their actions can make a difference in bullying situations.

GETTING HELP

Bullying is never OK. It's never the fault of the person who's being bullied. No matter how hard it might seem, there is always a way to stop bullying behaviors.

Talk to your parents and see if they can find ways to help you. Tell a teacher, counselor, or the school principal. It would also help to learn your school's policy on bullying. If there isn't a policy, talk to your friends, teachers, or other school officials about creating one.

There are many resources available to help people who are being bullied.

BE KIND TO ONE ANOTHER

STOP BULLYING

Helpful Resources

StopBullying.gov

www.stopbullying.gov

This government website has information on bullying and cyberbullying. It also has resources for getting help.

PACER's National Bullying Prevention Center

www.pacer.org/bullying

PACER's website is filled with interactive resources like videos with inspiring ways to stop bullying. They also have a website just for teens with a place to submit your own story.

What Should You Do?

Call 911 if someone is in a dangerous situation.

Call the National **Suicide** Prevention Lifeline at 1-800-273-TALK (8255) if someone is feeling hopeless or thinking of suicide.

Find a local counselor or **therapist** if someone is always sad, worried, or not acting normal.

LASTING EFFECTS

Bullying affects everyone: the person who bullies, the person being bullied, bystanders, and upstanders. The effects of bullying are different for each person involved. However, the effects are never positive.

People who are bullied are more likely to have poor physical and mental health. They may also do poorly in school and lose interest in things they used to enjoy. Bystanders are more likely to **abuse** drugs and alcohol later in life. They may also have mental health problems.

Bullying is a choice. Before you bully, think about how it will affect you and others. Instead of bullying, you can choose to walk away or be kind.

34

Bullying and Suicide

It may seem like bullying often causes young people to commit suicide. However, most people involved in bullying situations don't think about suicide. Even though they may not commit suicide, bullying still has lasting negative effects on them.

EFFECTS OF BULLYING ON PEOPLE WHO BULLY

People who bully are more likely to make bad choices—even as adults. They might:

- Abuse alcohol or other drugs
- Get into fights, destroy property, and drop out of school
- Get in trouble with the law
- Abuse other people in their life

CLIQUES VS. FRIEND GROUPS

A clique is a small group of friends who aren't friendly to others. Cliques usually have rules for being a member. People in cliques often use their control over others to exclude or be mean to outsiders.

Being in a clique can be miserable. You may have to dress or act a certain way. That can get very tiring.

Being part of a group is an important part of feeling like you have a place in the world. Friend groups often share a common interest. You're allowed to have different interests and be friends with people outside your group. In a friend group, people are free to be themselves.

DID YOU KNOW?

Boys and girls bully differently. It's more common for boys to physically bully others. However, it's more common for girls to verbally bully others.

HOW TO AVOID CLIQUES

- Do the things you like to do.
- Be true to yourself.
- Accept other people into your friend groups—even if they are different from you.
- Be an independent thinker.
- Stand up for what you believe in.

GOING TO A TRUSTED ADULT

If you are bullied or see others being bullied, speaking to a trusted adult should help. A trusted adult could be a parent or a teacher. They can make you feel better. They'll listen to you and give you advice. They'll also support you.

In therapy, people talk, do activities, practice new skills, and solve problems.

If the bullying keeps happening, then a counselor or therapist might be better able to help you. These adults are trained to help people with different problems. They will ask questions and listen. This will help them figure out how to help you.

DID YOU KNOW?

In the United States, about 20 percent of students 12 to 18 years old say they have experienced bullying.

TELLING VS. TATTLING

There are big differences between telling and tattling. Telling is when you want to keep yourself or someone else safe. The problem is serious. An adult needs to solve the problem. Tattling is when you want to get someone else in trouble or avoid getting blamed yourself. Safety isn't a problem. The problem can be solved without an adult.

Chapter 6

IMPORTANT LESSONS

Even though bullying is never OK, it can teach you important things. You know how bullying made you feel. Now you know how other people will feel if you bully them. Being bullied may also teach you that it's better to be who you are than be who people want or expect you to be.

Having strong friendships is important. A good friend will never bully you.

You might not be able to change how someone who bullies acts. But you can change your own thoughts and attitude. Try focusing on the positive things in your life.

DID YOU KNOW?

Bullying can happen at any age. Some adults experience bullying in their workplace.

BULLYPROOF YOUR FRIENDSHIPS

Bullies often target people who don't have many friends. The best way to prevent this from happening is to find good friends. Good friends:

- Treat each other with respect
- Are trustworthy and honest
- Aren't jealous of each other
- Defend each other
- Support other friendships

GETTING INVOLVED

There are many ways to help stop and prevent bullying. Many young people want to know what they can do to stop bullying at their own school. It's easy to get involved.

The Federal Partners in Bullying Prevention invite young people across the country to help stop bullying in their community. They have an online Youth Engagement Toolkit. It gives ideas for organizing bullying prevention events. You can also read about how other teens have gotten involved. More information can be found at:

http://www.stopbullying.gov

October is National Bullying Prevention month. However, bullying prevention should be a year-round effort. To prevent bullying, try including others or handing out positive messages on sticky notes.

NATIONAL
BULLYING
PREVENTION
MONTH

Chapter 7

More Confident Than Ever

I have positive messages posted on my bathroom mirror. They say things like, "Your interests make you interesting!" and "I can get through this." I look at them every day and feel a little bit better.

Middle school wasn't easy. But I started going to a therapist to talk about the problems I couldn't solve on my own. She taught me how to think positively and find the confidence to make friends.

My first year of high school, I still struggled with the popular girls bullying me. But I joined drama club and made a bunch of really great friends. However, I wouldn't have been able to deal with the bullying without some help.

Mia still faces challenges. But she has learned a lot about being confident and finding support when she needs it.

GLOSSARY

abuse: To use improperly or in harmful amounts. To treat in a cruel or harmful way.

aggressive: Showing a readiness to fight or argue.

counselor: A person who gives advice.

evidence: Something which shows that something else exists or is true.

exchange: To give or take one thing in return for another.

federal: Of or relating to the central government.

gesture: A movement of the body that expresses an idea or a feeling.

LGBTQ: Lesbian, gay, bisexual, transgender, and queer/questioning.

reflect: To make known.

reinforce: To encourage or give support to someone.

reputation: The way in which people think of someone or something.

stressful: Full of or causing stress, which is something that causes physical or emotional tension.

suicide: The act of someone who kills himself or herself on purpose.

taunt: To make fun of or say insulting things to someone to make that person angry.

terrorist: Someone who engages in terrorism, which is the use of violence as a means of achieving a goal.

therapist: A person who helps people deal with mental or emotional problems by talking about those problems.

threaten: To show an intention to do harm or something unwanted.

traumatic: Causing someone to become very upset in a way that can lead to serious mental and emotional problems.

INDEX